THE
VIETNAM WAR

THE VIETNAM WAR

VOLUME 12

After the War

Marshall Cavendish

New York · London · Toronto · Sydney

Reference Edition 1989

© Marshall Cavendish Limited 1988
© DPM Services Limited 1988

Published by Marshall Cavendish Corporation
      147 West Merrick Road
      Freeport
      Long Island
      N.Y. 11520

Produced by Ravelin Limited
Original text by Barry Gregory
Designed by Graham Beehag

Library of Congress Cataloging-in-Publication Data

The Vietnam War *70955500*

   1. Vietnamese Conflict. 1961-1975 – United States.
I. Marshall Cavendish Corporation.
DS558.W37   1988   959.704'33'73 87-18224
ISBN 0-86307-852-4 (set)
     0-86307-866-4 (Vol 12)

Printed and Bound in Italy by L.E.G.O. S.p.A. Vicenza

Contents

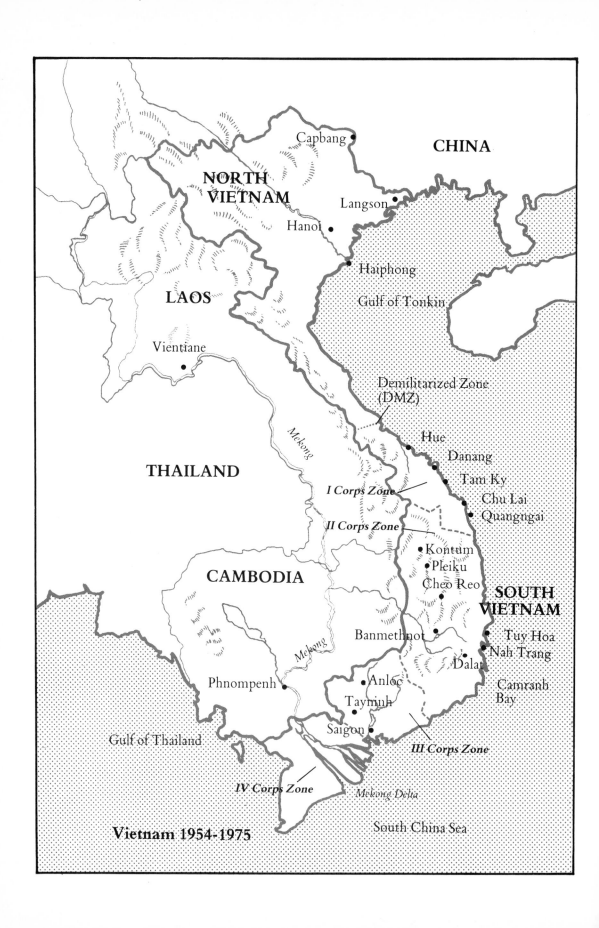

Vietnam 1954-1975

The Beginning of the End

When the Republic of Vietnam collapsed on April 30, 1975 and ceased to exist as a nation, the world at large — friend and foe alike — was taken aback. The rapidity and relative ease with which the Communists took over South Vietnam struck many people, even in the North, as something unbelievable.

U.S. military aid, and for eight years, the assistance of U.S. combat forces had helped the Republic of Vietnam build a viable force for self-defense. From an army of 170,000 equipped with obsolete weapons, the South Vietnamese armed forces finally emerged as a strong force, equipped with modern weapons, second to none among non-Communist Asian countries.

South Vietnam's air force ranked sixth in the world, and its best combat divisions rated as equal with their American counterparts. There is no doubt that the South Vietnamese soldier could fight, and he did fight well. But for years his efficiency and morale were based on U.S. combat support and the ever-ready supply of war materials from the U.S.

When the Communist Tet Offensive of 1968 had been smashed by the South Vietnamese Army and her allies, principally the USA, President Lyndon B. Johnson declared the Vietnam War a conflict America could neither win nor lose. He ordered the process of 'Vietnamization', which saw the gradual withdrawal of U.S. air, sea, and ground units over the next five years.

The Saigon government was not ready for the Vietnamization of its forces at that time, or any time later. Although the United States would be generous in the re-allocation of equipment ranging from aircraft, warships and tanks down to small arms ammunition, how could the South Vietnamese replace seven U.S. divisions, four

The initial success of the 1968 Tet Offensive, with the attack on the U.S. embassy in Saigon, signaled the political decisions to start 'Vietnamization' and American withdrawal from Vietnam.

brigades, and innumerable support units — in early 1968, well over half-a-million men?

The enemy's offensive of Easter 1972, when the North Vietnam Army and Viet Cong repeated the Tet-68 scale of attacks on over a hundred towns and cities of South Vietnam, brought to the surface the basic disadvantages of the Vietnamization process.

Although the ARVN with the help of U.S. airpower and mobility, again held the Communists, some territory was lost below the 17th parallel in the northern provinces of South Vietnam. Most areas lost remained lost for with the exception of Quang Tri province, it was beyond the capabilities of the South Vietnamese to take the ground back.

But still, as long as U.S. air power was available, the overall balance of forces could be maintained, and the Republic of South

The wreckage of an American B-52 triumphantly displayed in North Vietnam. The withdrawal of U.S. air support led to the final defeat of the South.

Vietnam stood a good chance of pulling through. Then came the turning point that changed the albeit precarious balance of power in favor of the Communists.

The Paris Agreement of January 1973, which had been the culmination of five years of often secretive negotiation between the United States delegation headed by Dr Henry Kissinger and North Vietnam in the person of Le Duc Tho, resolved only two issues — the immediate withdrawal of American forces, and an exchange of prisoners between North and South.

The Communists had clamored for Viet Cong representation in the South Vietnamese parliament, a proposal strongly resisted by President Nguyen Van Thieu. The president, who had been a leading ARVN general, was not a believer in a unified Vietnam. The Geneva Accords of 1954 had created two Vietnams — a

President Nixon deep in conversation with Dr Henry Kissinger, who headed the U.S. delegation to the peace talks in Paris, France in 1973.

Communist state in the North and a Democratic state in the South — and that is the way the majority of the South Vietnamese people wanted it to stay.

As the Paris peace talks had dragged on the Nixon administration came under tremendous pressure from the public at home to end the American involvement in Southeast Asia. Kissinger achieved just that — the last U.S. combat troops left Vietnam on March 29, 1973, and American prisoners-of-war, mainly airmen, were air-lifted home shortly afterwards.

The cease-fire began on January 28. President Thieu denounced the terms of the agreement as a sell-out by the Americans and was unwilling to add his name to the agreement, but he did so when President Nixon promised continued financial support.

Henry Kissinger accepted the Nobel Peace Prize for 1973, sharing the honor with Le Duc Tho, who declined to receive it. The Paris Conference had not brought peace to Vietnam; just another truce. The Communists claimed they had won a victory in Paris — with

Dr Kissinger and Le Duc Tho, head of the delegation of the Democratic Republic of Vietnam (North Vietnam) initial the agreement at the end of the Paris peace talks.

the Americans gone it would now be only a matter of time before the whole of Vietnam was turned into a Communist state.

If the 1973 Paris Agreement was the starting point for the demise of South Vietnam, and the absence of U.S. re-intervention was an encouraging sign to the enemy to proceed with the ultimate plan, it was the cutback in U.S. military aid that accelerated the whole process and made certain defeat inevitable.

After only a few months the Saigon government realized that unless the United States maintained its former level of supplies, the defense of its territories would at best be an uphill struggle. Nixon failed though to persuade Congress that the necessary funds should be made available and the impact of this reluctance to help further shattered South Vietnam's dreams of democracy.

Early in 1973, President Thieu set about reorganizing his defenses in South Vietnam, but this was no easy task. Generally speaking, the military situation at that time reflected a rough balance of opposing land forces but the loss of U.S. tactical air support tipped

One of the terms of the Paris agreement was that U.S. prisoners of war held in North Vietnam should be released and returned home. One such POW was Sergeant Jon R. Cavaini of the Green Berets.

the balance in favor of the Communists.

President Thieu's efforts at re-aligning his forces were hampered by the fact that numerous North Vietnam Army and Viet Cong units remained lodged in South Vietnam and civilians made homeless by the fighting in 1972 were a big problem.

The Paris Agreement had decreed that the future of Vietnam was to be 'gradually implemented through peaceful means'. There could be no doubt that for both North and South 'peaceful means' on the contrary meant 'at the point of a gun'.

The Peace that Never Was

Some measure of the haste with which Kissinger finally wanted to steer America out of the Vietnam War after five years of tedious and ambiguous negotiations in Paris may be gleaned from his imperious attitude to the South Vietnam government in the latter half of 1972 and a study of the terms themselves. Whereas the Agreement embodied the basis for peaceful reconciliation, no penalties were attached if either party deliberately chose to ignore the terms.

When on August 16, 1972 Dr Kissinger arrived in Saigon, he met President Thieu and explained the political pressures in the United States and the influence these pressures might have on the approaching U.S. presidential election. He also affirmed President Nixon's determination to seek a solution to the Vietnam War.

Then on September 11, Kissinger and Le Duc Tho met again in Paris. This time all clauses to which both parties had previously agreed were put on paper. In essence it was agreed that reconciliation in Vietnam should be based on mutual respect between North and South.

Both sides should stop seeking to eliminate each other. South Vietnam should not be forced to accept either a Communist regime or any pro-American regime. For the first time, the Communists refrained from demanding the removal of the Saigon government and its replacement by a coalition government.

As it had been prepared and agreed by Henry Kissinger and Le Duc Tho, the draft agreement covered nine issues:

1. The United States respects the independence, sovereignty, and territorial integrity of Vietnam.
2. The cease-fire was to be effective 24 hours after the agreement

North Vietnam's chief negotiator, Le Duc Tho. Both he and Kissinger were awarded Nobel Peace Prizes. Tho declined to accept his award.

was signed. All U.S. troops were to be withdrawn from South Vietnam within 60 days.

3. All prisoners were to be released within 60 days.

4. An administrative structure called the National Council of Reconciliation and Concord was to be created to organize general elections.

5. Reunification of Vietnam was to be implemented gradually through peaceful means.

6. An International Commission of Control and Supervision (ICCS) was to be established.

7. An international conference to guarantee peace was to be convened within 30 days.

8. All parties were to pledge to respect the independence, sovereignty, and territorial integrity of Laos and Cambodia.

9. The United States was to participate in the postwar reconstruction of North Vietnam and Indochina (sic).

The prospects looked good for signatures. Both sides definitely wanted a cease-fire before the U.S. presidential election in November

A Lockheed AC-130 gunship operating from neighboring Thailand. Their presence was cited by Kissinger as part of the guarantee of South Vietnam's independence.

(1972); the North Vietnamese especially, who were convinced that President Nixon would be less flexible if he was re-elected.

On October 18, Henry Kissinger flew to Saigon and met at the Independence Palace with President Thieu. Kissinger began the session by handing the text of the Paris Agreement, in English, to Thieu. The American negotiator then explained with emphasis the points he thought advantageous for South Vietnam.

The United States, he stressed, pledged to maintain its airbases in Thailand, and to keep the Seventh Fleet off Vietnam to deter any attack by the Communists. Economic and military aid would continue for South Vietnam while the U.S. believed that secret understandings with Soviet Russia and Communist China would seriously reduce the supply of war materials to North Vietnam.

Kissinger pointed out to Thieu that South Vietnam did have an army of over one million men and did control 85 per cent of Vietnam's nineteen million population. South Vietnam, Kissinger was confident, would develop and prosper in the postwar period. The agreement, the American negotiator concluded, was good.

> The U.S. military used up 27,000 tons of supplies for every day spent in Vietnam, 20 times the amount consumed by the enemy.

An aerial view of the POL (Petroleum-Oil-Lubricant) depot at Haiphong. America had mined this harbor to prevent supplies from reaching North Vietnam.

As part of the final pull-out of U.S. forces from the war zone large quantites of equipment and supplies were handed over to the ARVN. Here training is given on a 105-mm howitzer.

In Saigon, Thieu and his ministers recognized the proposed treaty as virtually a private cease-fire arrangement between the U.S. and North Vietnam. There was certainty that the Communists were not going to abide by the standstill cease-fire and Thieu showed Kissinger captured enemy documents that attested they had no intention of doing so.

Dr Kissinger's private scenario for the acceptance and signing of the agreement was clearly in jeopardy. He informed Le Duc Tho that the United States was prepared to sign the agreement on October 31. At the same time, North Vietnam was told that the mining of Haiphong harbor and bombing of pre-selected targets below the 20th parallel, which had been resumed in May, would cease.

For his part, President Thieu went on radio and television to make his point that the government of South Vietnam could not accept a coalition. Hanoi in turn denounced Thieu for undermining the 'peace proposals'. The Communists further demanded that the

agreement be signed on October 31, as requested by Kissinger.

During November, a major consignment of war materials arrived in Saigon by air and sea. The supplies included F-5 and A-37 fighters, C-130 transport planes, helicopters, M-48 tanks, and 175-mm artillery pieces. American bases and equipment were also transferred intact to the South Vietnamese armed forces.

The new weapons and equipment enabled the ARVN to form additional heavy artillery, armor, and anti-aircraft artillery units. Now F-5 and C-130 squadrons were formed. The deliveries had the dual purpose of supplying much-needed weapons to South Vietnam, and demonstrating that the U.S. was a reliable ally. President Thieu was still reluctant however to ratify the agreement.

On November 9, Kissinger's deputy, General Alexander M. Haig Jr, arrived in Saigon, and delivered a personal letter from Nixon to Thieu. In his letter, the American president stressed the significance of the Saigon arms consignment to the South Vietnamese president and stated that if Thieu was still reluctant to sign, the United States might go ahead separately and sign with North Vietnam.

The U.S. now found it difficult to get the North Vietnamese to the conference table in Paris. Nixon and Kissinger decided on a strong line, which set in motion on December 18, the 11-day bombing of Hanoi and Haiphong. B-52s flying from Guam and Thailand, as well as carrier-based naval aircraft, flattened the two areas in the most controversial bombing episode of the Vietnam War.

North Vietnam was forced by the 'Linebacker' raids to return to the Paris talks. Nixon and Vice President Agnew were inaugurated for a second term on January 20, 1973. On January 19 the South Vietnam government was informed that no more changes would be made to the agreement, which would be signed by all parties involved on January 27. The cease-fire would go into effect at 8.00 a.m., Saigon time, on January 28, 1973.

President Thieu did not have much choice in the matter. President Nixon informed him by letter on January 21, that if South Vietnam rejected the agreement, Nixon re-confirmed that the United States would sign separately with North Vietnam, and as a consequence all aid to South Vietnam would be cut off.

But if South Vietnam signed the agreement, the president of the United States would intercede more vigorously with the U.S. Congress for continuing aid to South Vietnam, and the U.S. government would 'react vigorously' to any serious violation of the cease-fire by the North.

> **The Vietnam war cost the U.S. an estimated $165 billion.**

Despite America's decision to withdraw from Southeast Asia final gifts from the U.S. of aid and produce arrived in South Vietnam. These pigs were given to some villagers on condition that they will later hand over some of the litter to other villagers.

Renewing the War

In theory, the Paris Agreement of January 27, 1973, ended the war in Vietnam. However, while true peace prevailed in the North, military conflict continued in the South. No clause in the Paris Agreement called for the withdrawal of Communist forces, nor was there any understanding about keeping them at bay.

The International Commission of Control and Supervision (ICCS), set up by the Paris Agreement, proved a total failure in enforcing the peace terms. The Communists quickly took the opportunity of launching a mammoth propaganda campaign to convert the South Vietnamese people to their cause.

Phase One was devoted to the propaganda teams, who aimed at convincing the Southerners in their rural homes that the Paris Agreement was in fact a Communist victory. Phase Two was the implementation phase. The Communist efforts would be suitably co-ordinated so that the South Vietnamese would actually rebel against the Saigon government.

Phase Three was the consolidation phase. If necessary the NVA and VC units would use military action to enforce the Communist doctrine. The Communists never attempted to conceal their planned course of action. As a result, on the first day of 'peace', more than 1,000 violations of the treaty were recorded.

During 1973, besides small-scale 'land and population grab' activities, the NVA launched four division-size attacks, in direct violation of the cease-fire agreement. The objective of all four attacks was to secure suitable areas, which could be turned into bases to support a major offensive.

By the end of 1974, the Communists had seven infantry divisions stationed in South Vietnam. Hanoi had formed two army corps

After January 1973 the defense of South Vietnam relied on the ARVN soldiers. Communist violations of the Paris treaty started from day one.

headquarters in South Vietnam's I Corps Tactical Zone, and one in III Corps. Also south of the 17th parallel were an armor brigade, an artillery division, an anti-aircraft division, two engineer divisions and a transportation group.

In July 1974, Danang in I Corps Tactical Zone was seriously threatened by two NVA divisions and an independent infantry force. In II Corps, the Communists began constructing two major roads eastwards from the Ho Chi Minh Trail. These highways gave easy access for Communist movements into the interior of South Vietnam.

In III Corps, the NVA used artillery effectively in the battle for the outposts. South Vietnamese troops were lured into pre-selected areas and pounded mercilessly with deadly concentrated fire. ARVN losses were heavy but they had some success with small assault teams in silencing the enemy batteries.

In the Mekong Delta, the South Vietnamese forces were generally on the offensive during this period. Large-scale 'search and destroy' operations were conducted by the ARVN supported by the Regional and Popular Militia Forces but the Communists were

A demonstration of Viet Cong infiltration techniques against ARVN positions by a former VC sapper.

nevertheless in control of many villages and hamlets in the Delta region.

President Thieu's defensive strategy immediately after the cease-fire had four major objectives. First and foremost, South Vietnamese forces were to keep the national territory intact and to maintain full control over the population. Second, the armed forces of South Vietnam were to be maintained at the maximum possible strength.

Third, the South Vietnamese would seek to improve and modernize their methods and weapons, which entailed building new roadways to carry troop transports and supplies, and improved firepower.

Fourth, the armed forces would continue to assist in the national pacification and development program and take part in other national projects — such as maintaining village defenses, farmland reclamation, and the re-settlement of refugees. South Vietnam's three goals were self-defense, self-management, and self-sufficiency.

South Vietnam's national economy was in a serious state with the increasing loss of foreign exchange, rising cost of living, and widespread unemployment. Defense expenditures remained, as they had always been, a major burden for the national budget.

Early in 1974, the South Vietnam government confirmed that oil had been discovered in the continental shelf of South Vietnam. This news naturally triggered a mood of optimism for the future of the country's economy. South Vietnam still hoped for a true peace settlement and gave no credence to the thought that the nation could be abandoned.

South Vietnam's General Cao Van Vien went to the United States in April 1974 to test the U.S. Congress's reaction to aid for 1975. Officials of the U.S. Department of Defense assured the general of their full support. Unfortunately for South Vietnam, though Congress authorized support to the tune of $1 billion, it finally appropriated only $700 million, which was well below the wartime levels of financial aid.

The South Vietnamese Air Force was hit especially heavily by the reduction in U.S. aid. Some 200 aircraft were put out of service. Four hundred jet and helicopter student pilots training in the United States were called home. Naval activities were reduced by an average of at least 50 per cent.

Riverine operations, which had featured so largely in the campaign in the Mekong Delta, were cut by 72 per cent. This huge reduction required the demobilizing of over 600 river craft and boats, 240 of which belonged to the Regional Forces.

The war in Indochina continues today — some 150,000 Vietnamese troops are still fighting in Cambodia (Kampuchea).

A meeting of Viet Cong and NVA in one of the liberated areas of the Mekong Delta.

The defense of remote outposts in the Mekong Delta and the security of military harbors in Danang, Qui Nohn, Cam Ranh, and Saigon and its environs were seriously compromised. Some attempt was made to improve the South Vietnamese Navy's sealift and amphibious capabilities, to assist troop movements in the event of a full-scale offensive by the Communists.

In the spring of 1974, after the New Year of the Tiger, a high-level conference of Communist officers met at 33 Pham Ngu Lao Street in Hanoi. Included were representatives from 'all the battlefronts, all services and branches, all corps and divisions, as well as representatives of all agencies of the General Command'.

The purpose of the conference, which was attended by President Ton Duc Thang, Ho Chi Minh's successor after Ho's death in 1969, was to review progress so far and to set the guide-lines for the conquest of South Vietnam. The right of the people of South Vietnam to self-determination was seen by Hanoi as the Communists' right to enforce their regime on the South, for the benefit of its people.

During the summer and fall of 1974, all the agencies of the

General Staff were bustling with activity, if a trifle tense. 'Warm breezes' from the South indicated to the northerners that the situation on the battlefield in South Vietnam was moving to their advantage.

For example, 'Zone 9', in the 'liberated territories', had 'grasped the concept of strategic offensive and defeated each of the enemy's encroaching operations, swept away more than 2,000 enemy outposts, and liberated more than 400 hamlets with a population of more than 800,000'.

Furthermore 'Zone 5' had 'gone more and more strongly on the offensive, expanded its bases in the border zone (Nong Son, Thuong Duc, Tuy Phuoc, Minh Long, Gia Vat, etc.), stepped up attacks against the enemy in the lowlands, wiped out nearly 800 outposts, and liberated 250 hamlets with 200,000 people'.

The 'enemy' in the opinion of the Hanoi leaders in late 1974 had become passive, and started to decline everywhere. Saigon's 'pacification and encroachment' plans had been significantly thwarted in many of the lowland areas, especially in the Mekong Delta.

The Northern Offensives

The first of the NVA campaigns which resulted in the fall of South Vietnam was aimed at the city of Phuoc Long, which lies 75 air miles from Saigon, in the III Corps Tactical Zone. The area bounded to the north by Cambodia was already used by the NVA for major base facilities.

The terrain is mountainous and blanketed by dense jungle which denied air observation. Phuoc Long City was linked to Saigon by two highways. One of these routes connected Phuoc Long with Quang Duc and Ban Me Thuot to the northeast.

The battle for Phuoc Long began in the latter part of December 1974 and ended on January 6, 1975. Saigon's attention was quickly turned to the III Corps crisis area and infantry reinforcements and weapons, ammunition and other equipment, were airlifted to Song Be, Phuoc Long City's airfield.

On the night of December 30, the NVA 7th and 3d Divisions launched an attack against the district town of Phuoc Binh. The attackers were supported by a tank regiment and artillery. The situation in the battle area rapidly deteriorated for the ARVN. Troop reinforcements were not immediately available and the enemy had cut land supply routes.

Although airborne Rangers were sent by helicopter to Phuoc Long on January 3, the city's defenders could not withstand the NVA main force of two divisions and its complements of armor and artillery. As one veteran Ranger summed up the battle: 'The enemy troops were not so good and so courageous as we might have thought. There were simply too many of them!'

The Communists meanwhile, were preparing for their next major campaign with more confidence than ever, encouraged by the

NVA soldiers with a Russian-made anti-aircraft gun. North Vietnam was moving towards victory.

new U.S. 'hands-off' policy. Indications were that II Corps Tactical Zone would be the launching pad of the offensive then in the making. By the end of January 1975, the NVA 320th Division based at Duc Co (near Pleiku) was reported moving toward the Darlac Plateau.

Other NVA divisions — for example, the 316th, the 312th, and the 341st — were reported moving southward, but their destinations were unknown to the South Vietnamese forces. The 316th Division in particular concealed its movement toward Ban Me Thuot by cautiously approaching from lower Laos.

The main thrust in II Corps was to be against Ban Me Thuot, the battle raging from March 10-18, 1975. In the preliminary phase, the NVA planned to cut Routes 14, 19 and 21 to sever the highland provinces from the lowlands, and by the same action block possible reinforcement routes for the ARVN.

The first prong of the attack on Ban Me Thuot was directed by tank-led infantry against an ammunition depot north of the city.

The second enemy effort was directed against Phuong Duc airfield where the enemy advance was at first held. The third and leading effort, another combined tank and infantry attack, swiftly overran the airfield and pushed into the city, establishing blocking positions as it moved.

During the night of March 10, the NVA 316th Division appeared on the scene and encircled Ban Me Thuot. Unfortunately, during a South Vietnamese air strike, a bomb dropped on a communications center. Communications with the city were lost from that time.

On March 13, the 7th Rangers were airlifted into Ban Me Thuot in an attempt to save the besieged city, by now under the virtual control of the enemy. An attempt was made to rendezvous the relief force with battered troops escaping from the nearby Phuoc An Garrison, but on March 18 Communist troops captured Phuoc An. The battle for Ban Me Thuot was over.

The North Vietnam Army had now carried out dress rehearsals in both II and III Corps Tactical Zones where they now occupied large portions of South Vietnam territory. The Communists had achieved their objectives by the use of superior numbers, and not least by serious tactical blunders by the South Vietnamese commanders.

After the fall of Ban Me Thuot the ARVN had little alternative but to withdraw from the II Corps highland region. The fall of the central zone took place between March 14 and April 2, 1975. Organized as a planned withdrawal, the 'redeployment' of ARVN forces from the highlands was turned into a rout by pursuing NVA units.

In theory each retreating convoy was a fighting column, which would stand and fight, but progress to the coast was hampered by refugees fleeing from the Communists, and road surfaces which were badly in need of repair.

The ARVN's evacuation of key base areas at Pleiku and Kontum had taken the NVA by surprise and several days elapsed before the NVA 320th Division was sent in pursuit. The Communists were equally hampered by the refugees, bad roads and the lack of intact bridges to cross rivers.

South Vietnam's defeat in the II Corps Tactical Zone was a psychological as well as a military defeat for the nation. Guilt weighed heavily in the politicians' minds and accusations and counter-accusations were rife in Saigon circles. Rumors of a deal with the North caused thousands of people to leave their homes in II Corps, as well as I Corps to the north.

Refugees and battered troops streamed south along the coast heading for Saigon. In the national capital itself, the government was fast losing strength. Confidence in the armed forces was at its lowest ebb.

Demonstrators angrily demanded the replacement of President Thieu; they also vigorously voiced anti-American feeling. A hope still lingered, however, for some miraculous thing to happen that would save South Vietnam.

Meanwhile in mid-March, the Communists had begun an all-out offensive in the I Corps Zone, directing their attacks against Hue

As the North Vietnamese began to occupy more and more territory in the South ARVN prisoners fell into their hands.

and Danang. The withdrawal of South Vietnamese I Corps forces was to be routed via Danang; they would be embarked on ships in the harbor.

Before dawn on March 29, a thick fog had set in along the coast. All available naval ships were at the rendezvous points as planned, but the tide was low, the ships could not beach, and the troops had to wade and swim toward the ships. When the ships left, over 6,000 Marines and 4,000 ARVN troops of the 3d Division and other units were on board.

With the Communist forces closing in to control I Corps the refugee problem increased every day. The wary people of Hue, which had lost over 3,000 of its citizens at the hands of the Party executioners after the Battle for Hue (Tet-68), began moving out in earnest on March 17. The city had already been abandoned by the military.

Route 1 southwards to Danang was packed with people and vehicles of all kinds. It was estimated in late March that over one and one-half million people were stranded in Danang with no escape routes open on land to the south. The refugees took over every public building, all the public roads, and the harbor. The chaos and disorder were indescribable. Hunger, looting and violence were widespread.

On March 27 came the first U.S. commercial jet chartered for the evacuation. It had been planned to airlift about 14,000 people in daily runs between Danang and Cam Ranh. But news of air evacuation spread rapidly. Soon Danang airport was besieged by a frantic crowd, deserters included, who trampled the security fence, overwhelmed the guards, swamped the runways, and mobbed the aircraft.

At Danang harbor another unruly crowd took over the piers. A number of U.S. oceangoing vessels arriving in Danang were ordered to anchor offshore. Then the refugees were taken by barges and small boats to ships. The operation was slow but it brought good results. As each ship had taken aboard 10,000 people, it was directed toward Cam Ranh.

During the night of March 28, the Communists shelled and vigorously attacked Danang. In the morning of March 29, the refugees continued to leave by barges and tugboats under the enemy's merciless fire. More casualties occurred as the refugees desperately swam away from the shore toward any floating vessel.

During the afternoon of March 24, out of sheer luck and audacity, a U.S. commercial airliner suddenly landed at Danang, took aboard 300 refugees, and took off to the consternation of

Thousands of refugees took to the highways to escape the Communists' advance.

Communist troops who did not know how to react.

By this time Danang had been occupied by NVA troops, and all evacuation efforts were officially stopped when the day was over. Still the refugees continued to make their way south by whatever means they could find in the days that followed.

The Fall of Saigon

Right: NVA tanks roll into Saigon. Their presence heralded the unification of Vietnam under Northern control.

Below right: A local Viet Cong hero, now out in the open, is welcomed by the village children.

Below: Fleeing ARVN troops ditch a Huey in the sea near the U.S. Navy task force assembled to evacuate as many people as possible.

The final NVA offensive, christened the Ho Chi Minh Campaign, was directed against Saigon on four fronts, on each by a force equivalent to a three-division army corps, or in more simple terms, about 200,000 men. The NVA were equipped with masses of tanks and artillery.

Saigon was situated in the extreme south of III Corps, and its commander, Lt Gen. Nguyen Van Toan, was considerably handicapped in his efforts to defend the city by in-fighting in the Saigon parliament. Many people demanded that the once popular President Thieu should resign and transfer his powers to Gen. Duong Van Minh.

A coalition government, it was argued, stood a good chance of being accepted by the Communists; if so further bloodshed could be avoided. On Monday April 21, during a meeting at the Independence Palace, President Thieu resigned, nominating Vice President Tren Van Huong as his successor. As it happened Van Huong's reign was short-lived and General Minh did in fact take over control in the last few days of the Saigon administration.

Some people believed that an immediate cease-fire – certainly within 24 hours – would follow Gen. Minh's inauguration. But for others who had never compromised with the Communists and for whom a coalition meant certain death, the inauguration of Minh was a signal to pack up and leave.

Practically every square mile on the approaches to Saigon was fought over with no quarter given by either side. Early on the 29th, the airport at Tan Son Nhut was devastated by enemy bombardment. At 10 a.m., III Corps HQ reported that the

Vietnamese civilians, under U.S. Marine guard, wait to be off-loaded from a U.S. merchant ship during the evacuation of April 1975.

Anxious children, some separated in the chaos from their parents, wait for news.

A U.S. Navy landing craft lies alongside the cargo ship *Sgt. Andrew Miller* to deliver supplies to the Vietnamese refugees aboard.

situation was critical. Ranger companies roamed the defense lines in desperate efforts to fend off the attackers.

Completely surrounded and isolated, left without support and without reinforcement, the Capital Military District waited hopelessly to be conquered. President Minh gave 24 hours for all U.S. civilians and personnel to leave Vietnam.

The evacuation had been carefully planned. The airlift by helicopter to ships of the U.S. Seventh Fleet proceeded feverishly throughout the night and was over by dawn of April 30. During that time over 1,000 Americans and 5,000 South Vietnamese U.S. employees and their families were lifted to safety.

At 10 a.m. on April 30, 1975, President Minh ordered the South Vietnamese forces to stop fighting and lay down their arms. And South Vietnam came under Communist control and no longer existed as a free nation.

Uncertain Victory

When on April 30, 1975, the Communists took over Saigon, the victors were not greeted with garlands of flowers. Crowds stared in dazed silence as tanks rumbled through the tree-lined boulevards. Many people were still trying to find the rendezvous point for American helicopters. And rumors spread around the city that ships would leave from one place or the other.

At first people came into the streets to watch the North Vietnamese soldiers out of curiosity. There was no voluntary demonstration to support the intruders. They came as foreigners and not as brothers. But after a few weeks, the Communists organized propaganda demonstrations and a lot of people turned out to see them because they were scared.

The Communists claimed total victory in South Vietnam and in the military sense no-one could deny it. But the South Vietnam Army had in the last weeks of the conflict broken up through inward chaos and despair. North Vietnam's triumph had like all successful offensives in modern war been won through weight of numbers before a shot was fired.

The Communists held a victory parade in Saigon, now named Ho Chi Minh City, on May 15, which marked the day when a reign of terror commenced to subject the South Vietnamese people to Communist rule. Some onlookers were puzzled by the absence of Viet Cong flags. When questioned northern officers shrugged their shoulders and replied that the VC were now 'integrated' with the mainstream Communist forces.

It was not until July 2, 1976, that Vietnam was officially united as the Socialist Republic of Vietnam (SRV). By this time the National Liberation Front (the Viet Cong) had been disbanded, and

Children raise a Viet Cong flag in the early days after the fall of South Vietnam. Such flags soon disappeared as the VC were 'integrated' into the NVA.

the Communist administration, remaining in Hanoi, retained a distinctly northern flavor amongst its representatives.

The Viet Cong (Cong is short for Cong-san, which means Communist in Vietnamese) had become a potent guerrilla force as early as 1959. The movement consisted of two wings. The political arm was known as the National Liberation Front (NLF) and the military arm the People's Liberation Armed Forces (PLAF).

Both were directed by the People's Revolutionary Party (PRP), the southern branch of the Vietnamese Communist Party, which had received directions from Hanoi through the Viet Cong's headquarters in the III Corps sector on the Cambodian border.

In fact, not all the Viet Cong were Communists. Many owned land and businesses in South Vietnam, and merely represented an opposing faction to the former Saigon 'regime', which like the North had come into being after the Geneva Accords of 1954.

The Viet Cong, without whom the North would never have conquered South Vietnam, resented the exclusion of their flag from the Saigon victory parade. Moreover, non-Party VC were angered when they were not re-united with their families, homes and businesses, as Hanoi had promised once the South had been overrun.

This move was just part of a ruthless policy to punish the South for its past freedoms and to purge southern society of all known opponents of Communism. This would be carried out by wholesale executions, 're-education' for the less dangerous, and the re-location of others' from towns and cities to the countryside.

The new over-lords' objectives were not merely to impose a Socialist state, in which the rich were taxed and ridiculed but to institute a truly Communist police state in which no-one was allowed to conduct any form of business, own property, or keep a bank account.

At the top of the list for purging were the 'intellectuals' — civil servants, lawyers, doctors, business men, teachers and priests, etc., whether they were actively opposed to Communism or not. The Hanoi government dared not risk freedom of speech in the south.

Many Catholics and Buddhists could not hold gatherings or ceremonies in churches and temples. Communist-indoctrinated Buddhist monks arrived from the North to take over in the temples. Those Buddhist priests who resisted were brutally tortured and murdered. Some were buried alive.

Teachers sympathetic with the former republic were arrested. The Communist Party sent in new teachers from the North to take over the schools. They created party cells to convert those teachers

New Communist militias, armed with Chinese weapons and Lenin-style caps, were raised as part of the iron rule imposed on the South. This one is from Saigon (now renamed Ho Chi Minh City).

who would co-operate. The Ho Chi Minh Youth Movement, not unlike the Hitler Youth of Nazi Germany, was formed to spy on teachers, family and friends.

Children in kindergarten and primary schools were taught marching songs and told stories about children in the North who had died and been maimed in the American bombing raids. They were encouraged to draw Communist soldiers on their note-pads. In arithmetic lessons the pupils were posed questions like: 'There are 30 American bombers in the sky and 20 are shot down. How many are left?'

The noose tightened in June 1975 when all adults were forced to register their names for 're-education' and were subjected to

interrogation about their past activities. Foremost amongst them were former military and civil servants.

One former government official, who later escaped to the U.S. has described how people were lined up outside a public building, under the watchful eyes of North Vietnamese soldiers armed with automatic rifles.

Once inside, a Communist team commenced by telling the assembled people to remain 'calm and receptive'. Then the officials began reading out charges against them non-stop for four days. The people were urged and then threatened to 'tell the truth' — confess their crimes, and denounce their friends.

Public executions were carried out in the streets of Saigon. Even children were shot for making rude gestures at Communist soldiers. Dissidents filled the jails where conditions were inhuman. Prisoners were kept in tiger-cages and brutally beaten.

Many former politicians and even Viet Cong were kept in these prisons. It is said that some 200,000 guerrillas had deserted the Communist ranks during the war. By the end of 1975 those who had been identified had been executed or imprisoned.

Then after the initial purges in Saigon, the Communists shifted their attention to the countryside, where their savage practices were less likely to be seen by foreign observers.

Buddhist priests loyal to the Communist government parade through the streets of Ho Chi Minh City. Many suspected of disloyalty were killed.

The Brainwashing Machine

Many former South Vietnamese volunteered for 're-education' on the understanding that the program would last ten days. Little did they know that the Communists would keep them in labor camps for five years or more and thousands of prisoners would die in captivity.

Countless camps were built in the forest areas of South Vietnam. Prisoners were assembled in the Saigon area and transported to over 20 remote regions. Prisoners were used to clear the jungle to build new camps where living conditions were little better than in the jails.

Some of the larger camps were divided into sub-camps housing different categories of prisoners, including women. The inmates were allowed to receive letters but very often relatives and friends did not know which camp they were in. Visitors were not allowed in the camps.

One prisoner reported after his release that he had helped to build camps using cement donated by a Western country to help re-build Vietnam. Similarly food packages received from foreign countries did not find their way to the prisoners. But they were often used to feed the Communist guards.

The day in a 're-education' camp started with a meagre breakfast — not the rice Vietnamese would expect to eat but some cereal normally used to feed pigs. Many prisoners slowly died of starvation and there was not enough medicine to cure the stomach pains caused by the inferior food.

From 7 a.m. to early evening, the prisoners worked in the forest. In the dry season trees and underbush were cleared and burned to farm the land. The ashes from the burnt wood acted as a fertilizer and the soil could produce a good rice crop, which was used to feed the Communist soldiers.

The machete and a crudely-shaped hoe were the principal tools. Crops would be reared for one or maybe two years and when the top soil was finally washed away by the rains, the plots were abandoned. The Communists made good use of the stricken areas for propaganda purposes. They blamed the wasted paddy fields on defoliation with chemicals dropped from American aircraft during the war.

The evening in the labor camps was devoted to brain-washing. The indoctrination teams read from Communist texts. If the prisoners asked questions this was taken as prevarication and even insubordination. The sessions dragged on late into the night and only ended when the prisoners 'agreed' with the explanations of the Communist creed.

If the captives openly disagreed with the lecturers they were removed to a 'discipline house' where they were also sent if they disobeyed their guards. Here the prisoners were kept in complete darkness and in chains often for many months. For serious offenders there were Special Camps from which the captives were lucky to emerge alive.

International observers arriving in Vietnam knew about the 're-education' centers but they were not shown the real labor camps. In one place a visiting team was shown a 'show place' with comfortable dormitories, lounges, a hall for a cinema or theater, tennis court and a volleyball court. It was later used to house soldiers.

Many former members of the National Liberation Front were kept in these camps. These men were tortured and forced to sign confessions stating they had collaborated with the previous regime. Many of these men fought the French, the South Vietnamese, and the Americans. They were exhausted with the years of war and held no hope for the future.

Some of the prisoners were 're-educated' successfully by the Communists and the younger ones found their way into the new Vietnamese Army. The total identity of the ARVN had been eliminated after the fall of South Vietnam. The Communists built an army of over one million men, the fourth largest in the world, which was used mainly to protect Vietnam's border with China and to wage war in Cambodia.

In 1979 there was a conference on Vietnam held by the Red Cross in Switzerland when the Communists promised to release a number of prisoners. Some, after their families found the money,

Young Montagnards organized by Hanoi into a Communist youth movement.

left the country and others were sent to work with their families on farms in the New Economic Zones.

These New Economic Zones, which were formed in the south after the Vietnam War were groups of poorly equipped farmsteads

Despite the New Economic Zones, life in the countryside in the rest of the new, united Vietnam was often hard.

where city and town's folk were sent to make a new way of life. Most of these unhappy people had no knowledge of farming and were totally unsuited to life in the country.

Again the Communists picked out the 'intellectuals' whose continued presence in the urban areas posed a special threat to the Communist Party machine. Hands more used to the pen were soon wielding the machete and hoe clearing the jungle areas to grow crops on temporary farming lots.

As the workers toiled, Communist guards stood over them and graded their efforts. If the work was to the guards' satisfaction the workers were given a little rice — barely enough to subsist on. Whole families were put to work in this way, and it was the grandparents and the young children who were the first to die, mainly from malaria and starvation.

By 1980 many young people were escaping from the New Economic Zones. Some managed to return to the towns and cities where the police failed to find them. Others joined the 'boat people' who were still leaving Vietnam when the opportunity arose and they could find the money to pay to board the boats.

Building a Nation

The age-old objective of unification of Vietnam had been achieved in name only. Since 1975 harsh methods have been used to 'pacify' the south and mold it in the Communist pattern. In spite of help from Russia and China, the cost to Hanoi of waging war in the South had been enormous.

Much of the industry in the North had been devastated by American bombing, and life, always austere since Ho Chi Minh proclaimed the new republic in 1954, did not improve after victory in the South. Disaffected with China, the new Vietnam had to rely heavily on economic aid from Russia.

Many stories are told of how surprised even senior NVA officers were to find that everyday life in Saigon was not as bad as the Communist Party officials had made out. One NVA colonel visiting relatives immediately after the fall of Saigon was bewildered, to put it mildly, at seeing the standard of living enjoyed by many Saigoners.

The Communist move in 1978 to deprive the people of private means changed all that. In March all private businesses were confiscated in South Vietnam. In May a currency reform wiped out most private savings.

The black market which had flourished in the American days re-appeared in Saigon. Not so plentiful perhaps as previously, the market places became a great attraction from 1978 to the Russians, who had taken over Vietnam's new off-shore oil interests. Russian naval vessels were now frequently seen in southern harbors.

The Russians earned the sobriquet 'Americans with no dollars', but they still had plenty of money to spend. While stocks lasted the Russians eagerly bought goods the Americans left behind: Japanese

In the ten years following U.S. withdrawal, an estimated 1 million refugees fled Communist Vietnam. The exodus continues

transistor radios, wrist watches, textiles and especially jeans.

The corruption of Saigon re-occurred in Ho Chi Minh City and seemed to afflict northern civil servants sent south on duty. The party officials responsible for rationing sold some food legally but disposed of most of it on the black market.

Ten years after the unification of Vietnam, the one fact of life was poverty throughout the nation. The economic growth rate of 2 percent was poor compared with the predicted 14 percent in the Communist five-year plan of 1975. Furthermore, average personal income had dropped from $241 a month in 1976 to $153 in 1981.

The monthly meat ration quoted in the early 1980s was one pound per person. Two pounds of beef on the black market cost a month's wages. The staple diet for a day is a handful of rice, corn and vegetable. The huge quantities of rice produced in the south, which had been such a profitable export under the French, now goes to Russia in return for Russian financial aid.

The main aim of the Communists in the Indochina and Vietnam Wars was to rid the country of foreign domination and support. Because of its poverty however and its diplomatic isolation from China, Hanoi has been forced to rely on Russia not only for financial aid but expertise also in re-building factories, laying new roads, and equipping and training its army.

Ten years after the war ended the Soviet Union assisted Vietnam roughly to the tune of $2 billion a year, a drain on the over-burdened Soviet economy. The aid to Vietnam is essential but resented. Oddly enough for all the military aid sent to the North in the Vietnam War, the Russians treated the conflict as a side-show. Moscow even put pressure on Ho Chi Minh to take his hands off the South and concentrate on keeping his own state in order.

The friendship treaty signed between Vietnam and the Soviet Union in 1978 granted the Russians the right to use Vietnamese harbors and rivers. This suits not only Soviet naval vessels on maneuvers in fareastern waters but also trawlers allowed fishing rights off the Vietnamese coast.

In return for oil, fish, rice and an army capable of confronting Russia's not so friendly Chinese Army in South China, Russia perhaps has not too bad a deal with Vietnam in return for the financial aid and expertise for the country's development program.

North Vietnam's rift with China dates back over the centuries. When invading armies crossed the border from China, colonization took place. Just as the early English settlers in North America

A trader in Ho Chi Minh City after the Vietnam War. In 1978 the Communist government outlawed all forms of personal wealth.

eventually turned against their motherland, England, and won their independence, so the Chinese immigrants in Vietnam enjoying their colonial status, turned against the 'old country'.

A curious situation arose when the Communists finally conquered South Vietnam. A large number of ethnic Chinese had settled in the populated areas of South Vietnam, where their skills and business expertise had made them not only prosperous but valuable members of the community.

The northern Communists, although themselves basically of Chinese origins, despised the Chinese 'colonials' down south and after 1975 planned to eliminate them. China however, stepped in and invaded Vietnam in 1979 to conduct a two-month campaign, February-March, in which the result was inconclusive and huge losses were suffered by both sides.

In mid-1979, the Chinese in the south began fleeing by overland

routes to China where 260,000 of them were settled in the southern provinces. The reason they were able to leave so easily was that Vietnam was prepared to let the refugees go at a price. For a time trading in Chinese refugees was one of Vietnam's principal sources of revenue.

The Hanoi government set up offices to collect fees and bribes, often paid in gold and to confiscate the refugees' property and other possessions. Appeals were made to Chinese communities all over the world to help and checks poured into the Bank of Vietnam by the thousand.

The exodus of the Chinese, and approaching one million 'boat people', and the Communist purges left Vietnam short of manpower, expertise and skills that the new state could hardly afford to be without. A dark cloud was fast settling over the land, which now seemed as distant to Westerners, as it had appeared to the explorers of long ago.

A ferry carries an assorted load of passengers over a river in Vietnam. A good proportion of them are soldiers.

The 'Boat People'

The aftermath of the Vietnam War is marked indelibly in western minds by the plight of the 'boat people': the refugees who put to sea often in unsafe vessels to find new homes in foreign lands.

The saga of the Vietnamese boat people of the mid and late 1970s was not unique to their history. Nearly a million of them had fled North Vietnam when Ho Chi Minh formed the new Communist state in 1954. The great majority escaped by boat in any vessel that would float — down the South China Sea to South Vietnam.

The second wave of boat people commenced with the fall of Saigon in April 1975. The early refugees who had converged on Saigon were carried out by American transport planes, which had flown in military supplies in the hope of strengthening the defense of Saigon. These flights began on April 5 taking the refugees to Clark Air Base in the Philippines.

Then, on April 23, six days before the final evacuation of Saigon, a fleet of additional planes was called into service and began to take Vietnamese refugees to the island of Guam. Some 2,500 persons a day were brought to Andersen Air Force Base and the U.S. Naval Air Station on Guam.

On May 7, American and Vietnamese warships and cargo vessels, and a few small Vietnamese ships, arrived with more evacuees. By May 14, there were more than 50,000 refugees on the island. Although military and commercial aircraft were transporting the Vietnamese from Guam to the United States at an average of 1,000 a day, the arrivals far exceeded the departures.

The next exodus of Vietnamese people was between mid-1975 and late 1977. At first while the Communist officials were busy imposing their system on the south, escape by boat at night-time

A crew member from the ship *Cap Anamur II* carries a Vietnamese 'Boat Baby' to safety. The child was one of 52 rescued from the small boat in which they had escaped from Vietnam.

was quite easy. Then in early 1976, when the authorities having executed or detained South Vietnamese persons of standing and influence, forced the ordinary folk to register for 're-education', the scramble to escape mounted swiftly.

The boat people left their homes with whatever possessions they could carry and made their way with the stealth of guerrilla fighters through the jungle to the Delta river banks and coastal beaches. The boats they boarded would have made the average seaman shake his head in amazement. The money the refugees carried would be paid to dishonest agents, who would put as many people on board the boats as possible. And in storms and bad seas the boat people drowned by their thousands.

The available craft were small, always overcrowded, and not intended for long journeys. They headed nevertheless for ports in Thailand, Indonesia, Malaysia, Singapore, and Hong Kong. Their plight drew the world's attention to the boat people. The hazards of the journey were more than those thrown on them by the uncertainties of the weather in the unpredictable South China Sea. Many tales were told of inhumanity, terror and cruelty.

Horrific stories were related of the barbaric pirates operating in the Gulf of Thailand. The pirate boats under the guise of rescue vessels would tow the small boats, bulging with refugees to uncharted, off-shore islands where they were robbed, beaten and assaulted.

On one occasion, New Year's Eve, 1979, three boats of refugees totaling 190 persons sailed into the Gulf of Thailand and were set upon by four pirate boats. The pirates, wielding clubs, beat some of the Vietnamese men and then ordered the survivors to swim toward the uninhabited island.

Some of the women refused to head toward the island, and the pirates began throwing babies into the water until the women started to swim. By the time they had reached the island, there were only 120 of them left. The women ran away into the bushes, and the pirates followed them, hunting them down and assaulting them. The horror continued for five days before Marines from Thailand arrived on the island and rescued the terrified survivors.

There are no accurate figures as to the death toll of the boat people. But stories told by the survivors indicate that between 40 and 70 per cent of the people who left Vietnam by sea did not arrive elsewhere, victims of a merciless ocean and the cruel regime which forced them to flee. The Vietnamese dead may total as many as 400,000 persons.

The boat people who survived were not always made welcome

by the Southeast Asian nations, which cited economic problems, racial problems, and health hazards, for not wanting the refugees at all. It was even argued that the escapees were cowards, who had run away from the fight against Communism!

In 1979, Malaysia refused entry to some 55,000 boat people, and Indonesia had deployed a 24-vessel task force to prevent the Vietnamese from reaching Indonesian soil. All cited the same pressures — problems in feeding and housing the refugees, fear of racial conflicts resulting from the arrival of new people, and the fear of becoming involved in an armed conflict.

By July 1979, Vietnamese refugees, most of them ethnic Chinese, were leaving their homeland at the rate of 65,000 per month. In late July, 50 nations met in Geneva for a two-day conference on the situation. The meeting was significant because it established the principle that helping refugees should be considered an international responsibility.

Out of the meeting came pledges to the United Nations High Commissioner for Refugees for the Indochina program amounting to $190 million. The total permanent resettlement pledges by countries other than the United States were substantial: France, The Netherlands, Belgium, Britain, West Germany, Norway and Australia taking significant quotas of immigrants.

The Chinese exodus commencing in early 1978 marked the final phase of the mass departures from Vietnam. For the Chinese who hesitated in their decision to leave, China's invasion in February 1979 made up their minds for them. It was a matter of 'go' or be executed by the Hanoi Communists.

In late 1979, international banking sources in Hong Kong estimated that the money paid to the Vietnamese government for the release of the Chinese refugees averaged about $90 million per month. Thus the Hanoi government was doubly glad to see the Chinese choose to leave — their departure brought the government money and rid the country of a group the Vietnamese Communists wanted 'out' for a number of reasons.

In spite of Malaysian opposition to the refugees, by 1980 well over 100,000 were settled in camps in Malaysia. In Singapore the refugees' condition was almost idyllic by comparison with other camps.

Conditions were also good for those who were eventually allowed into Indonesia where there were refugee camps near Singapore, and in the Jakarta suburbs. The Vietnamese boat people who found refuge had one significant advantage over those who had

> **The Vietnam War cost the Government and people of the U.S. $1,000 million and 58,000 lives.**

The Boat People were both young and old. The refugees' departure from the country, frequently at great expense, helped raise money for the Communist government and also got rid of a number of 'problem' citizens.

fled overland to Thailand.

While the land refugees were in camps at least a year and in some cases longer, the boat people were processed in a matter of months. Their eventual journey to a permanent home was virtually assured once they reached the Philippines, Malaysia, Singapore, Indonesia, or Hong Kong.

Long before the boat people came to Hong Kong, the bustling and prosperous British Crown Colony on the southeast coast of China had its refugee problem.

For decades Hong Kong had taken in thousands of refugees from Red China and was hampered by shortages of housing and strained social services. Hong Kong has a total area of 400 square miles but the majority of its population of five million lives in less than 90 square miles of urban area.

By January 1980, there were some 55,000 Indochinese refugees in camps in Hong Kong where they were settled in four camps — Sham Shui Po, Jubilee, and Kai Tak North and Kai Tak East near Kai Tak Airport. The refugees, who were a mixture of ethnic Chinese and Vietnamese Buddhists and Catholics, were well clothed and fed and many of the adults were found jobs.

The refugees also at first fared well in Singapore where some were allowed to stay permanently. An island connected by a causeway to the Malaysian mainland, Singapore houses Malays, Chinese, Indians, Eurasians, Arabs, and English; the influx of Vietnamese adding significantly to the island people's culture.

But in October 1978, the Singapore government restricted the number of refugees arriving on Singapore soil at any one time to one thousand, and none of the new refugees could remain on the island for more than 90 days. After October 1978, getting into Singapore on anything but a foreign-flag vessel became virtually impossible for the refugees.

Cambodia and Laos

Following the Communist victory in Vietnam in 1975, Hanoi was swift to exert its influence over neighboring Cambodia and Laos. Cambodia had severed relations with the United States during the period 1965-69. Prince Sihanouk became increasingly convinced that the Communists would win in South Vietnam and allowed the North Vietnam Army and Viet Cong to use Cambodian territory for sanctuary and redeployment. By 1969 some 40,000 to 60,000 Vietnamese troops were in Cambodia.

The presence of Vietnamese troops in Cambodia was soon regarded as a threat to national sovereignty. In January 1970, Cambodian military forces began limited military operations against the Vietnamese in northeastern Cambodia, Prince Sihanouk abdicated and Cambodia was declared a republic.

Beginning in early 1970, Vietnamese Communist forces moved out of their sanctuaries to begin an invasion of the entire country. In Peking, to which he had traveled, Sihanouk formed an exile government with the support of Communist China and North Vietnam.

A government existed in Phnom Penh, the capital of Cambodia, until early in 1975 the Khmer Rouge (anti-government Communist forces) occupied the city and the five-year war was ended. There followed the mass killing of non-Communist peoples in Cambodia.

Gradually postwar chaos gave way to a degree of order under Communist control. An army-dominated constituent assembly drew up a new constitution that went into effect on January 5, 1976, and renamed the country Democratic Cambodia (Democratic Kampuchea).

Sino-Vietnamese Border War 1979

CHINA

Capbang

Dongkhe

Langson

Hanoi

Gulf of Tonkin

4 Vietnamese Divisions Stationed

LAOS

Vientiane

Hue

THAILAND

Bangkok

17 Vietnamese Divisions Stationed

KAMPUCHEA

Gulf of Thailand

Phnompenh

Ho Chi Min City

South China Sea

Vietnam and Her Neighbors 1979

During 1977, Vietnamese forces and the troops of Premier Pol Pot, who had ruled Cambodia since 1975, fought minor skirmishes along the border of the two countries. In January 1978, Vietnam sent forces deep into Cambodia in what they claimed was a move made to subdue Cambodian terrorist activity in the Parrot's Beak area of Southern Vietnam.

A Vietnamese soldier armed with an anti-tank missile, brandishes the weapon he used during his service in Laos.

Some of the Vietnamese troops were former soldiers of South Vietnam, who had been 're-educated'. By late December of 1978, Cambodia and Vietnam were locked in an all-out war. Nearly 100,000 Vietnamese troops, along with an estimated 20,000 anti-government Cambodians, had control of nearly a quarter of the country.

The fighting in Cambodia did not help the South Vietnamese refugees. This war had in turn created Cambodian refugees. In June 1979, Thai troops forced 42,000 Cambodian escapees back across the border. The Vietnamization of Cambodia followed harsh rules. Villagers were rounded up for forced labor and non-Communists obliged to flee into the jungle where they formed guerrilla bands.

The Vietnamese-controlled People's Republic of Kampuchea (PRK), in 1982, authorized the re-settlement of hundreds of thousands of Vietnamese civilians in Cambodia. They went to work in farming, fishing, lumber and handicrafts. In December 1983, Laos and Kampuchea signed an agreement with Vietnam to link the banking and economic systems of the two countries.

In 1949, France had confirmed the autonomy, or nominal independence, of Laos within the French Union. Prompted by the Communist-Viet Minh rebellion in Indochina, France granted Laos full sovereignty in October 1953.

Viet Minh troops, sided by members of the Pathet Lao (Lao Country), were already fighting in Laos, however. Despite the Geneva cease-fire of 1954 and another agreement, in 1957, for Laotian re-unification, fighting continued and the Communists held their territory.

In 1962 the three Laotian factions – conservative, neutralist, and Communist – agreed to establish a coalition government under Prince Souvanna Phouma. Fighting broke out again in 1963, and it was to continue sporadically into the 1970s.

As the war in Vietnam intensified in the 1960s, the situation in Laos worsened. In eastern Laos, the Ho Chi Minh Trail, North Vietnam's supply route through Cambodia into South Vietnam, was repeatedly subjected to heavy bombing.

On February 21, 1973, following the Vietnam cease-fire, Souvanna Phouma's government and the Pathet Lao signed a cease-fire agreement. A coalition government was again formed with Phouma named as premier.

With the Communist victories in Cambodia and South Vietnam, in April 1975, the Pathet Lao secured virtually complete control of Laos. Late in 1975 the Pathet Lao flag was adopted as the national flag, and on December 3, 1975, the monarchy was declared dissolved and the People's Democratic Republic of Laos was established.

The agreement between Vietnam, Kampuchea, and Laos of December 1983 thus joined together the old French colonial empire in Southeast Asia as a Communist union after 40 years of war.

Khmer resistance fighters who are still in action against the Kampucheans and Vietnamese.

Lest We Forget

About 900,000 people left Vietnam during the years 1975-85. Most of them were southerners. In Vietnam, to throw yourself on the mercy of neighboring countries was a calculated risk. The plight of the refugees was none worse than those who lived in the camps on the Thai-Cambodian border. Caught in the Communist struggle to take over Cambodia, the refugees held out little hope for the future.

The United States obviously had a special sympathy for the Vietnamese. The U.S. was particularly generous in financial aid contributed through the international agencies, and, through a number of domestic programs, providing additional assistance to those who came to settle in the country.

In April 1975, President Ford made available $100 million in U.S. Agency for International Development funds for assistance to Vietnamese refugees. Shortly after, the Indochina Migration and Refugee Assistance Act of 1975 authorized assistance to or on behalf of Vietnamese refugees under the terms of the Migration and Refugee Assistance Act of 1962. Assistance to refugees living in the United States was initially authorized through September 30, 1977, then extended, and was also provided for adult education programs.

The fall of Danang and Saigon saw many brave exploits by American pilots air-lifting orphaned children to safety in the United States. Amongst these a DC-8 of World Airways, a non-scheduled airline engaged in flying contract missions between the U.S. and Vietnam, brought out 57 orphans and their escorts from Tan Son Nhut airport, Saigon.

The flight was unauthorized and the DC-8 took off in defiance of the air traffic controller. The plane flew non-stop to Oakland,

Vietnam is today still a very poor country, where even the children have to work, such as here in a textile mill in Hanoi.

Even ten years after the end of the war some children's playgrounds are still bullet-marked buildings and rusting artillery cases.

California, where news of its arrival had been flashed beforehand. More than 500 people were waiting at Oakland airport to greet the arrivals, many of whom were adopted on the spot. This was the first of many such flights to arrive in the United States.

When however the first mass exodus of Vietnamese occurred, the attitude of the American public at large was unwelcoming. America's long and frustrating military involvement in Vietnam, was undoubtedly responsible for an initial feeling of indifference – even hostility – towards the refugees.

A Gallup poll taken in May 1975 indicated that Americans were opposed to admitting Vietnamese refugees by 54 per cent to 36 per cent. A front-page article in the May 22, 1975, issue of *The Wall Street Journal,* titled 'Vietnamese Refugees Find Starting Anew is a Frustrating Ordeal', gave many reasons, including the high unemployment rate and the language barrier, making resettlement difficult.

Immigration procedures were nonetheless established to allow 50,000 refugees per year into the United States for permanent residence. Statistics published in 1980 revealed that 316,000 Vietnamese persons were living in 51 states; California, Texas, Pennsylvania, and Washington being the largest areas of re-settlement.

For ten years Americans tried to forget the Vietnam War. The Watergate scandal in 1974 took greater hold of public interest, followed by the resignation of President Nixon. The great majority of Americans had no more been touched by the aftermath of the war and its consequences than were touched by the war itself.

An event as traumatic as the Vietnam conflict must have left wounds for those directly involved that time will never heal, and the tragedy was that the United States for many years seemed reluctant to face the issue at all.

Sympathy was undoubtedly aroused when veterans were seen in wheelchairs but often the returning vet found it difficult to adjust to civilian life in a society out of sympathy with the War.

Then in the early 1980s Vietnam somehow re-appeared as a subject for debate. Responsible books and magazine articles about the war were appearing and moreover were being read by the general public.

Movements sprang up to study the war and a Harris poll of 1980 taken amongst Vietnam veterans declared that the majority believed in the war and did not regard themselves as 'victims' of the state.

> **After the U.S. left Indochina, Khmer Rouge revolutionaries killed an unimaginable 2 million people in Cambodia (Kampuchea).**

> **Half a million Americans still suffer the effects of the war. They have a nervous disorder called post-traumatic stress.**

Opinions varied as to the significance of the war, and still do, but hard thought began to be given to the historical facts, particularly those leading up to American combat involvement.

Were Presidents Kennedy and Johnson right to assume that any delay in U.S. involvement in Southeast Asia would be seen by future historians as the same kind of appeasement on the part of Britain and France in compromising with Nazi Germany at Munich in 1938, a sinister event that did not prevent the world from being plunged into total war?

After World War II, America, traditionally isolationist whilst its people built a prosperous nation, occupied a new status in the world. The U.S. was now leader of the Free World and a new enemy had arisen — Communism. Did America respond appropriately to the Communist challenge in Southeast Asia? And, as it transpired, was the nation right in leaving South Vietnam to its fate?

Vietnam issues will be discussed for many years to come but apart from relatives of the dead, the misery of the permanently disabled, heartache remains for other groups of Americans. Foremost amongst these are the families of the missing-in-action (the MIAs).

Since the end of the Vietnam War, more than 2,500 American servicemen remain missing in action in Southeast Asia. Of these men, 166 are known to have been captured alive. In one case — that of Navy pilot Ron Dodge — his photograph appeared four months after his capture in the French magazine *Paris Match*.

Ron's wife Janis never received a letter from him but it still came as a shock when his name was not included in Hanoi's list of POWs to be released in 1973. Janis Dodge had already made the trip to France to lobby the North Vietnamese delegates at the Paris Peace Conference confronting them with her husband's photograph in the *Paris Match* article.

The story has an ending. In July 1981, Hanoi decided to return Ron's body; along with those of two fellow pilots, Richard Van Dyke and Stephen Musselman, both of whom were also known to have been captured alive. The only conclusion can be that all three were killed by the Communists. The question remains. Have some of the remaining Americans been converted to Communism? Many believe that most of those still living are being held against their will.

Another problem that lingers is that of the Amerasians fathered by American servicemen. A few of the lucky ones have been traced by their fathers and now live in the United States. The vast majority of them though are considered outcasts in Vietnamese society.

A continuing reminder of the War are the large numbers of children of mixed American and Vietnamese parents still in Vietnam.

An American journalist visiting Vietnam in 1983 reported that many of these youngsters were to be seen begging in the streets. They were generally good-looking kids who spoke excellent English. They considered themselves in every way to be American. The Vietnamese have been uncooperative in dealing with the Amerasian problem; the young people face a dismal future.

For the North Vietnamese victory has been at best a bittersweet affair. In terms of its essential war aims, the Communist regime has to a certain extent been a loser.

A Communist Union exists in Southeast Asia with Vietnam virtually in control of Cambodia and Laos. On the other hand, the region is now one of the poorest in the world. The legacy of victory for the Vietnamese has been one of disappointed dreams and great suffering. The goals of the 30 Year War have been achieved only partially if at all.

Glossary

ARVN	Army of the Republic of South Vietnam.
Boat People	Refugees fleeing Vietnam by boat.
ICCS	International Commission of Control and Supervision.
NVA	North Vietnam Army.
Pathet Lao	Laotian guerrillas.
PRK	People's Republic of Kampuchea – the post-1982 name for Cambodia.
SRV	Socialist Republic of Vietnam – united North and South Vietnam.
Viet Cong	Communist guerrillas.

Index